Dog Blessings

ALSO BY JUNE COTNER

Amazing Graces
Animal Blessings
Baby Blessings
Bedside Prayers
Bless the Beasts
Bless the Day
Christmas Blessings
Comfort Prayers
Family Celebrations
Forever in Love
Graces
The Home Design Handbook
House Blessings
Looking for God in All the Right Places
Miracles of Motherhood
Mothers and Daughters
Pocket Prayers
Teen Sunshine Reflections
To Have and To Hold
Wedding Blessings
Wishing You Well

Dog Blessings

Poems, Prose, and Prayers Celebrating
Our Relationship with Dogs

EDITED BY
JUNE COTNER

New World Library
Novato, California

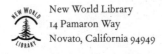 New World Library
14 Pamaron Way
Novato, California 94949

Copyright © 2008 by June Cotner

For permission acknowledgments, see page 157.

Text design by Tona Pearce Myers

Library of Congress Cataloging-in-Publication Data
Dog blessings : poems, prose, and prayers celebrating our relationship with dogs / edited by June Cotner.
    p.   cm.
Includes index.
ISBN 978-1-57731-616-9 (alk. paper)
1. Dogs—Literary collections. I. Cotner, June.
PN6071.D6D62 2008
810.8'03629772—dc22   2008024973

First printing, October 2008
ISBN 978-1-57731-616-9
Printed in Canada on 100% postconsumer-waste recycled paper

 New World Library is a proud member of the Green Press Initiative.

10 9 8 7 6 5 4 3 2 1

Contents

1. A Dog's World

2. Puppies

3. Our Bond

4. Devotion

5. Aging Gracefully

6. Partings

7. Reflections

8. Prayers, Blessings, and Inspiration

A Letter to Readers

What would the world be like without dogs? Who would be there to walk with us at night, protect us, play with our kids, share our joy in life, and teach us how important it is to smell everything before engaging with it?

My life has been measured and defined by my dog companions. When I was a child, my black cockapoo, Pixie, was always by my side. My mom died when I was eleven, and I remember many nights crying into Pixie's soft fur. Pixie would look at me with the most compassionate expression — as though she understood that I was devastated.

As a young adult, my two golden retrievers, Sundance and Shalimar, came into my life. Sundance, the male, was reserved, noble, and dignified. Shalimar, the female, boiled over with enthusiasm. She died suddenly of unknown causes at age eight. My heart broke as I watched my four-year-old son place a Band-Aid on one of her eyes to "make her better." When we buried Shalimar in the backyard, Sundance curled up on her grave and let out a mournful howl. After Shalimar's death, I wrote a poem, "Shalimar's Golden Rules," which is framed in my office and includes the line, "Never turn down a tummy rub!"

A little golden fur ball named Peaches soon joined our family. And a year later came Thunder, a German shepherd. He had an extremely loyal, "at your service" demeanor and followed me wherever I went. In contrast to Shalimar's gusto and enthusiasm, Peaches was incredibly calm and frequently curled up with our white cat, Cali.

And now, Mary and Allante, my dear senior-citizen dogs, lie by my feet as I work. They give me gentle nudges and earnest gazes when it's time to go out, time for a treat, or time to be petted. Given their present sleepy-time days, it's amazing to reflect back on their very destructive phase as rambunctious youngsters. My friend Roger once took a look at all the holes in our backyard and said, "These aren't dogs. They're gophers in dog suits!"

In *Dog Blessings*, you will find poems and prose that reflect every phase of a dog's life, from the fun of watching a zesty young puppy at play to our utmost compassion in caring for an elderly dog. I've selected poems that eloquently show how dogs bring blessings to our lives in countless ways: from their loyalty and faithfulness to their help in raising kids, from watching them feel everything full blast to laughing over their many quirks, from their unconditional love to their steadfast devotion.

Dogs invite us into their world, and through that, our lives are deeply enriched. The poems and prayers in *Dog Blessings* celebrate our love and devotion for dogs, which in turn is reciprocated many times over by *their* love and devotion for us. As one of the early readers of my book said, "If you don't own a dog now, after reading *Dog Blessings*, you will want to adopt a dog right away."

One of the most painful realities of being a dog owner is that we will most likely outlive our canine companions. The pieces in the "Partings" chapter brought great comfort to me for the dogs I have lost, and I hope they will for you as well. Other chapters in *Dog Blessings* (such as "A Dog's World," "Our Bond," and "Prayers, Blessings, and Inspiration") celebrate the exuberance of loving a dog.

There is much we can learn from dogs. Dogs go with the flow of life. If they have to go live in a new home or with new people, they accept it, adapt easily, and become happy in their new environment. If they lose a leg in an accident, they learn to run with three legs. When they become old, they take it easy and don't feel sorry for themselves. Many people wish they could be as good as their dogs. I know I do.

You have likely picked up this book because you are a dog lover. I have endeavored to make *Dog Blessings* a loving tribute to the kindest, most caring and devoted animals known to humankind. I hope I have succeeded.

June Cotner
P.O. Box 2765
Poulsbo, WA 98370
june@junecotner.com
www.JuneCotner.com

Thanks

Dog Blessings would not have become a reality without the love my dogs have given me throughout my life. My agent, Denise Marcil, knows how important dogs are to me and suggested creating a collection that would celebrate, honor, and dignify the deep respect for the blessings that dogs bring to all of our lives.

But it takes a lot more than love and passion to bring a book to fruition. I'm deeply grateful to my editor at New World Library, Georgia Hughes, who was equally enthused about this book idea. My appreciation also goes to the other folks at New World Library who have worked on *Dog Blessings*: Munro Magruder, associate publisher and marketing director; Monique Muhlenkamp, publicity director; Kim Corbin, senior publicist; Kristen Cashman, managing editor; Mary Ann Casler, cover designer; and Tona Pearce Myers, type designer and compositor.

Many thanks go to my husband, Jim Graves, and my daughter, Kirsten Casey, for being the first eyes and ears for the hundreds of submissions that were considered for the book. Deep appreciation goes to Laura Judson for typing the comprehensive test-market manuscript.

After I selected my favorite pieces for the test-market manuscript, a panel consisting of dog lovers and poets gave me their feedback regarding the final selections that appear in the book. Specifically, I'd like to thank my husband, Jim Graves; my sister, Susan Cotner; and my friends, Lynn Eathorne, Patricia Huckell, and Dale and Sue Peterson; all of them provided excellent input.

To ensure that my selections were of the highest literary quality, the following poets, whose work has appeared in a number of my anthologies, lent their expertise and gave me a careful critique regarding the possible selections for the book: Barbara Crooker (author of *Line Dance* and *Radiance*), Arlene Gay Levine (author of *39 Ways to Open Your Heart*), Donna Wahlert (author of *The First Pressing*), Mary Lenore Quigley (author of *Indelible Ink*), and SuzAnne C. Cole (author of *To Our Heart's Content*).

Dog Blessings would not have become the book it has without the inclusion of outstanding, heartfelt work from poets who have contributed to my anthologies for many years. In creating this book, I was also pleased to consider work from hundreds of newer poets who responded to my call for submissions in *Poets and Writers*. Thank you so much for your treasured words! Please visit "Meet the Contributors" at www.JuneCotner.com to read a short bio on each contributor. Special thanks also go to Rev. Nancy J. Cronk for forwarding my call for submissions to all her colleagues at www.Inter faithOfficiants.com.

And last, I'm grateful to God for bringing the myriad blessings of dogs to our world.

CHAPTER ONE

A Dog's World

SKIJORING WITH KANE

The world is a large bay of wonder
and here we are, circling the snow-covered golf course under
the ribbon wisps of moonlight — you, mutt with glacial
blue eyes and oil black fur, and me, a girl on skis
skating behind you, seeing your feet kick
through shadows of spruce
and elm. I let go
so that fear waddles on the outskirts
of the golf course parking lot. I let go
because the harnesses connecting our bodies
are taut and stretched and we race
the night, we speed faster than the lone car
passing the adjacent boulevard. Kane, dog of my heart,
if you reach heaven before I do
don't wait for me — run to the distant cloud edges,
let your feet rumble and shake free
a snow storm spiraling toward earth, toward
the winter girl watching from her window, remembering
ice, remembering the soft, swift pads
of one dog's feet.

Stephanie N. Johnson

QUEEN OF CANINE CAPERS

Of mischief-making she's accused,
Our queen of canine capers.
She's masterful at chewing shoes,
And shredding Sunday papers.

Destructor of our flower beds,
Disturber of our sleep,
In spite of all her troubling ways,
Her company we keep.

She often begs to be let out
To take her doggy walks;
Yet once her leash is snapped in place,
She disobeys, and balks.

Our midnight piddler of puddles,
A pooper of the piles,
Creator of huge messes, but
Her antics bring such smiles.

Her face appears quite innocent
Each time that she's chastised;
But careful observation shows
Rebellion in her eyes.

She has a sort of impish grin,
If you can call it that,
Appearing on that face of hers
Each time she steals my hat.

Though loving and affectionate,
Her playful puppy ways
Can wreak such household havoc as
To make one feel quite crazed.

Of course we love her anyway;
There's no way one could not.
So please, dear Lord, our patience grow,
A little, no, a lot!

Susanne Wiggins Bunch

GOOD DOG

When I walk the dog I let the dog
decide where we go. I keep the leash loose
and follow in her footsteps to the busy street
that scares us both, but it's the only way
to the grand tree at the corner where she stands
in a trance, her nose vacuuming the bulging roots
for a snoot-full of who-knows-what.

Sometimes she heads the other way, to the empty lot,
a minefield of turds I step through gingerly
while she throws herself on the foulest ones
and spins like a washing machine agitator,
then trots to the puddle by the curb and takes
a long drink, lapping it up like champagne,
splashing as if it were the fountain of puppyhood.

Her shanks and feathers drenched and dripping,
she looks at me as if I envy her
and seems to say, *Okay, I'm good and wet
and camouflaged in the scent of excrement,*

let's go home now and I'll slip beneath your desk
into a dream of running squirrels into trees
and you take the heat for letting me get into everything.

Eric Nelson

OFF THE TRAIL

The dogs are going crazy, running
in eddies around and around
circles getting wider

their heads and tails bobbing
against the sky — out of sight
back again.

The smaller dog's tail
long and tipped white
serves as a fish bobber

to show where the line of dogs
pays out against the currents of wheat.

They bark and yap
in huge bursts of sunlight,
ground soft and green
under their pads.

There is something about dogs
loose as wind that lifts the heart

as they run, fling themselves
over hills and hummocks,

you forget about paths and long to follow
off the well-trod and into the whisper
of grasses practicing free verse.

The dogs are frenzied with all they must fit
into their moments, their necks free
of leashes, their legs given to whatever strides
they choose. They race so fast, with such

buck and canter, that a new smell
jerks them almost off their feet.

They poke their noses without caution,
drink it in as if it were brandy.

When have we last given way to smell,
lingered to draw it into the nose, let it run
warm as liqueur down all the senses of the body?

When has a smell been so grand
we have longed to roll in it,

as the black dog does now,
four legs flailing at air, tongue lolling,
head dancing side to side,

all the full-out running and leaping
abandoned to this?

CB Follett

MOTHER OF DOG

I want to buy him
a lunch pail
notebook paper
pencils, and
some spiffy kid clothes.
Instead I buy him a T-shirt that says
RESPECT THE NOSE.
I'll teach him the new math,
the old rules for playing with others.
He'll be the envy
of all the mothers.
He won't stick chewing gum under his desk.
He won't pass notes in class.
He might eat his homework.
For him, life is recess.

Kelly Cherry

AT LIMANTOUR BEACH

The old dog celebrates.
Sniffs high. Races to the water
and runs a tight circle in the shallows,
two, three, and then another.
She lowers her shoulder
to an irish green swatch of sea lettuce.
She will roll in it, if she can,
if we let her, and wear it
as a badge of this day.

A day she always dreams of, by the fire,
legs churning on the rug — a beach day.
She can never get enough. Every beach
is another notch in her dreamtime.

She selects a rock, smoothed and oval,
carries it dangling from her mouth
like a talisman.
It is a digging rock. She drops it.
Chases it with her paws, poking her nose
in to scent its trail.
Her gray muzzle is thick with sand,

her legs, and around her eyes.
Her tongue is sandpaper, coarse grit.

By the third hole, she must sink to rest
every eight paw strokes, or so,
haunches perched on the slag of her own mining.

We spend the whole day at the beach,
marking the water's edge with a long line
of holes and heaps.
Tonight, while she runs
before the fire, the tide will rise
and replace all her divots.

CB Follett

WHEN DOGS GO ASTRAY

Where are you tonight? Chasing night critters
in the woods, eating food left on a patio

for felines on the lam, sleeping on a stranger's
patio cushions? I find comfort only

in knowing that you are together, my phone number
woven into your collars. I'm puzzled. How did

you get out of our fenced backyard? Did
some workman checking phone or cable lines leave

the gate ajar, just enough for you to make a break
for it when he wasn't looking? O Bartleby!

O Melville! Why couldn't you have been content
to smell unfamiliar shoes, to accept a pat on the head

or to protect our yard from an intruder? You're not
West Highland Terriers for nothing, born to hunt,
born to follow rabbits and rodents to their secure dens,
oblivious to your own needs in the heat

of the hunt. I have to believe you'll turn up
on someone's back step, begging to come inside

a stranger's house. Please choose a dog lover who
won't keep you from those who wait for your call.

Rosanne Osborne

DOG RUNNING WITH HIS MAN

For the sleek golden retriever, it is relief,
this bounding along the shore with his man.
Most of the time, it is all he can do to keep
his nerves within his skin, being assaulted
as he is every second of his life with
gorgeous smells, a constant heady flooding
from the world. It rushes at his too-keen nose:
sea salt, dead fish, rich green weeds
left behind by fingers of tide.
So much! The tingling edges of pine forest,
urines sprayed on every tree, sweet
sting of dung, bird tracks and tracks of other dogs
pressed lightly in wet sand, a bit of salami
to the left, dropped from a picnic, faint wood smoke
from a distant bonfire, and oh, the high he gets
from a whiff of female canine musk. Impossible
to know what to do with such happiness,
what he perpetually wants but can barely bear.
How it propels his fast, muscled flanks,
makes his ribs heave, his tongue pant.

At the end of the run, the man bends down,
offers a *good boy*, pats the young dog, his simple
loyal companion, never knowing
all that he carries, all that he craves.

Joanne Esser

DAISY

She has not
turned Lassie / Rin Tin Tin
to save us from
certain death.
She's never been featured
on *Animal Miracles*
or the evening news
for rescuing a child from a fire,
preventing a car crash, or
running impossible miles
to tell some former owner
that he is in trouble
or to ask why he abandoned her.
She has never
collared a criminal,
although she's spent time in a cell
for the sin of being homeless —
a menace to the public,
running at large,
begging and unruly,
matted hair dragging from her back legs,
beard as wild as an Old Testament prophet's.

Sentenced to death at the county shelter,
she was reborn, got a second chance
to visit wild places
and roll in piles of leaves,
discover new scents on wooded hikes,
and occasionally get into the trash
because everybody's entitled
to a little backsliding
now and then.

Karen R. Porter

WHAT? YOUR DOG DOESN'T TALK?

Mine does. Mine talks a blue streak.

Has a full English vocabulary, colloquial and formal,

uses simple and complex sentences,

and muscular prose,

accompanied by a full range of gestures, tricks, and expressions.

Grammatically iffy sometimes, but always deeply felt.

A fine sprinkling of Italian and Yiddish, too.

Here is a sampling:

- Welcome to our house. I'm Miss Molly. See. It says so on my chair.
- Mom, can you believe it? This guy won't get out of the car. He thinks I look fierce. Ha. Ha. Ha.
- I prefer THIS chaise lounge (chair, rug, hole) right now, and if I turn around three times first, it'll be even more perfect. Ain't life grand?
- I'm really, REALLY sorry, Mom. I didn't feel well.
- Move over, would you? And by the way, I was here first.
- I'll come when you show me the goods.
- Okay then, if I lie down and put my face on the floor between my paws, will you PLEASE give me some?
- Are you upset, Mom? Here. Let me love you . . . put my head on your thigh . . . lick your face . . . rub your nose

... put my paws around your neck ... make you laugh with a genius antic. Or we can just sit here, if you want.

- *G'valt!* What's THAT? It moves. It's WAY too big to be a dog. A horse, you say? Well, I don't care what it's called, I'm staying away from it.
- Are you talking AGAIN about what a great dog I am? Talk on, and I'll listen and thump.
- Ummmm. Get a load of these lilacs ... carrion ... goose (horse, dog, rabbit) poop ... new mown grass ... fish ... birds ... air ... the weird smell in the hallway. Life is delicious, and smells SOOOOOO great.
- Okay. If I can't come, I'll just wait here until you get home.
- Oooooh! I just LOVE it when you brush me ... tickle my ears ... rub my belly ... my hind quarters ... that place on my back ... no, not there! THERE!
- Ahhhhhhh! This is the life.

Fran Dorf

SWEETER THAN HONEY

Our dog has developed an addiction
to paper. It started innocently enough with
the dirty tissue a woman walking just ahead of us
accidentally dropped in his path one day.
Much to his delight. Not long after this,
he discovered dinner napkins, toilet paper rolls,
and book jackets. Most recently, I caught him
nosing around in our green clay pitcher that
used to contain all one hundred and fifty psalms,
typed up and individually folded like so many
fortunes, waiting to be read. One by one
he is making his way through the songs of thanksgiving,
prayers of lament and hymns of coronation.
Always careful to leave enough time
for three daily naps, a chew on his bone,
and the occasional bark at our neighbor's daring cat.
*How sweet are your words to my taste, O God, sweeter
than honey to my mouth.* To which I say: *A-hem.*

Lisa Dordal

OUTSIDE, WANTING IN

His paw a blur of motion
scratching on the screen.
Outside, wanting in.
Door opened, he bounds
across the room, tail beating greetings,
nuzzling us, tongue dangling,
circles twice, thuds to the floor
at our feet, sighs, relaxes content.

Until...
a vagrant squirrel hurls insults from the oak
or a supercilious cat twitches right across
the lawn that belongs to him,
or a mysterious shadow slants
across the porch perhaps signaling danger.
At once he's up again, barking,
crashing pell-mell to the door, pawing,
glancing imploringly over his shoulder.
Inside, wanting out.

SuzAnne C. Cole

THE SCIENCE OF FAITH

Every day except Sunday for five years
Sal tossed my dog a treat as he delivered our mail.
Then he was promoted to a desk job.

It's been months since Sal delivered
but when the dog hears the little white truck
coming up the rise, she still runs to the mailbox.

There she waits as the truck drives to the end
of the road and turns around, the white tip
of her tail whipping the air faster and faster

as it comes back her way, her whole body
wiggling with joy when the mailman stops,
sticks a handful of mail in the box, then

nothing.
The tail slows to a sway,
slows even more as the truck pulls away.

There she stands
head turned to the empty road
tail still as the pendulum of an unwound clock.

My husband calls it operant conditioning.
I say it's the science of faith,
hope stirred by memory and desire.

Patti Tana

LOST DOG

It's just getting dark, fog drifting in,
damp grasses fragrant with anise and mint,
and though I call his name
until my voice cracks,
there's no faint tinkling
of tag against collar, no sleek
black silhouette with tall ears rushing
toward me through the wild radish.

As it turns out, he's trotted home,
tracing the route of his trusty urine.
Now he sprawls on the deep red rug, not dead,
not stolen by a car on West Cliff Drive.

Every time I look at him, the wide head
resting on outstretched paws,
joy does another lap around the racetrack
of my heart. Even in sleep
when I turn over to ease my bad hip,
I'm suffused with contentment.

If I could lose him like this every day
I'd be the happiest woman alive.

Ellen Bass

UNLEASHED

Oh you are a beautiful flash of purpose
as you race toward the geese,
scattering them, every one. The wide
arc of their furious flapping, their loud
squawking, their berating, their clamorous
lifting is like great bells of hammered brass
ringing out in the Church of Brave Terriers
on The Day of Infinite Bones. And you,
my brown and white bullet burning with joy,
you are magnificent as a ringer of bells.
Please, allow me to be your student,
let me learn to be as purely alive as you.

Ginny Lowe Connors

DOG OUTSIDE A GROCERY ON BROADWAY

It was how he waited
how he waited where somebody told him to wait
how he paced outside the grocery store
how he tugged on the leash tied to the signpost
how he looked at the man coming out of the store
how he looked at the glass door swinging shut
how he looked at the man tearing cellophane off a pack of
    cigarettes
how he looked at the cellophane falling on the sidewalk
how he looked at the girl stuffing a red purse in her pocket
how he looked at the old lady opening an umbrella at the
    crosswalk
how he looked at the boy who looked at him through the
    window of a bus
how he looked at the bus turning the corner out of view
how he sat down on the sidewalk and got up again
how he pushed his nose against the glass door
how he scratched behind his ear
how he waited

Joan I. Siegel

CHAPTER TWO

Puppies

PUPPY DOG WELCOME

Bunny-hop gallop,
with dance-happy eyes,
Fly-swatting tail,
with glad-you're-home smiles,
Snort-like greetings,
with padded-paw embrace,
Slobber-lick kisses
planted all over your face.

Joan Marie Arbogast

PUPPY DAYS

Bless this frisky puppy
Who's into everything
His playful fresh behavior
Is like a day in spring

Remind me to be patient
When he's chewed another book
Or races through the living room
With a newly laundered sock

He loves without condition
Gives me kisses every day
And greets me with a wagging tail
After I have been away

Like any other baby
He needs a lot of rest
When he falls asleep curled next to me
I know that I am blessed

Louise Webster

HIGHER LEARNING

I put him out four times this morning,
let him fetch the paper, walked him
round the block, but still the puppy
peed twice on the kitchen floor —
great, spreading puddles of gold
that soaked into the doormat.

He looks at me with the eyes
of an assistant professor up for tenure,
hopeful about his classroom evaluations,
his latest research. If nothing else,
he thinks we should retain him for his warm
collegiality and service to the institution.

But he is merely plotting where to poop next.
No limit to the academic freedoms
of a dog these days, no end
to the publication of alimentary happiness.

Paul Willis

HIS

My puppy's small cries
have crept beneath the sill of my sleep
like such sad little crickets
that I have had to
spring him from his crate
and take him into my bed.
With the soft pads of his paws
pressed to my nose
I smell puppy smell
until we both wag ourselves silly
and he yawns a big puppy
my-head's-too-heavy yawn
and curls himself about my head.
In this gentlest of coronations,
I am crowned — His.

Linda Opyr

WALKIES

He scorns my gait
That eager pup,
Content to wait
Till I catch up.
There isn't room
For any doubt
Who's taking whom
When we are out!

John Bennett

CHAPTER THREE

Our Bond

HOMECOMING

Whether I've been halfway around the world or just out to the mailbox, Jenny's greeting upon my return is equally enthusiastic. I hear her prepare for my arrival as I walk across the garage. First, there's the gentle thud as she leaps off the couch in the family room above me, then the clicking of toenails as she races across the tiles on the kitchen floor, and finally the thawp-thawping of her sturdy tail against the walls in our tiny mudroom. By the time I open the back door, Jenny's tail is moving so fast and furiously, her entire body is wiggling and waggling. She leans into me, nearly taking me out at the knees as she does so, as though she just can't get close enough. She looks up at me, golden eyes shining with pure joy. It's always a perfect homecoming.

Christine Otto Hirshland

RESCUE DOG

I often wonder just who rescued whom.

Ostensibly, I am the rescuer. I searched for weeks to find just the right dog who most needed me. I filled out detailed adoption papers and drove a hundred miles to meet his foster family. When they decided we were a good fit, I brought him home, where I provide for his basic needs and then some, showering him with attention and affection. In short, I welcomed him into my home and my heart.

In return, he gives me dozens of reasons to smile or laugh each day. He greets me enthusiastically when I return from a long absence — say, five minutes or more. He endeavors to be my constant companion, shadowing me as I go about my daily routine and always available should I need a smooch or a snuggle. In short, he brings joy and laughter and love to my life.

So you tell me — who rescued whom?

Sonya R. Liehr

LOVE AT FIRST SIGHT

I wandered by cages lining the room
Sad eyes pleaded, *Please pick me.*
How can I choose?
Heartbreaking task
Wishing I could adopt them all
Then I saw him
Brown eyes peering at me from
under salt and pepper brows
Long dirty hair, beard crusted and messy
Stub of a tail wriggling his rear
Soft pink tongue reaching through grating
to lick my hand
"I'll take this one," I said
and named him Addison
For 15 years my furry friend and I
played, romped, cuddled
Truly cared about the other
I learned to love so much stronger
so much better, so much truer
because of one special little dog.

Millie Ruesch

COMFORT ZONE

We have our spot.
Each night she waits for my
"Say-up," flying weightless
Into a clump of soft hair
Warming my feet up on the couch.
Slipping into the comfort of
Old marrieds, content with
Nearness and routine.
I reach down and squeeze her foot
In our secret shake. She eyes me,
flops over, sighs.
God is nigh.

Janice A. Farringer

THE GREETING

I open the door.
You are already
bounding to the door
with a wagging tail,
flashing teeth,
and four prancing paws.
Your healing power dissolves
the most difficult day
from memory.
A cold nose
and warm kisses
trigger a child's laughter
from my heart.
I am a better human
for having you
in my life.

Joan Noëldechen

COMPANIONS

Maybe it's that old story of rescue
Lassie. Rin Tin Tin,
the two dogs and the Siamese cat
on a long walk back, looking for home.

Or it could be a fixed point in the day,
sureness of warmth, need,
a timetable, yes
a timetable.

It's not an easy world, as we all know
You turn around and you are old,
or sick, or hurting; reaching out
to whatever reaches back.

Feathers and fur talk of the now,
keep us humble in the minute,
because they must be fed,
walked, played with
in exchange for a love
that has no limits.

Immune systems may be erratic,
the very planet may wobble,
yet this day begins with a squawk,
a bark, a wet tongue.

I open my eyes; I am alive.

Lynn Martin

DOG DAYS

My dog days are over. I had just buried Lord Buffington's collar along with a large dog biscuit. Buff was a remarkable golden retriever I had rescued from a shelter fifteen years earlier. His cheerfulness had carried me through five orthopedic surgeries. Now, still on crutches, adopting even an adult dog seemed more than I could handle. *Besides*, I consoled myself, *I will never love another dog the way I loved Buff*.

Then Taffeta entered my life. Morris, an older gentleman who traveled a lot, asked me to look after his beautiful, parti-colored cocker while he was away. Apprehensively I agreed, and soon realized I *could* care for her because of her "Velcro" cocker nature — she would not leave my side. I found myself looking forward to Morris's trips, warning myself not to get too attached because she and Morris were moving to the West Coast.

Taffeta broke through my pall of loneliness and, despite my admonitions, that fall, when Morris went on a trip around the world, I fell in love with her. I remember the moment: She was curled up on her red plaid bed and, as I walked by, something happened to my heart. I had owned dogs, horses, and ponies all my life, but I'd never felt a love like this before.

When Morris died unexpectedly, Taffeta became my dog. She changed my life. How can you be depressed when the cutest cocker in the world wiggles her entire body in delight when you say, "Want to defrost the refrigerator?" Scratching those downy ears took the morning stiffness out of my hands. Her "motorized" tail-wagging gave me the incentive to get up.

Sadly, after four years, illness again shattered my world. Despite superb veterinary care, Taffeta died of non-Hodgkin's lymphoma. But she had taught me an important lesson: No matter how much you loved a previous dog, no matter how devastated you are when he dies, you *can* love another dog.

Nancy A. Messinger

OUR DOG

She's our source of entertainment,
Great affection and delight.
She's our guardian protector
Through the long and cold, dark nights.

She's the licker of our faces.
She's the chewer of our shoes.
She's a loving source of comfort
On the days we have the blues.

She's our under-table taster.
She's the sensor of our moods.
She's the great appreciator
Of our kitchen table foods.

She's the filler of so many roles
That make our life so sweet.
Without her in our family,
Life would not feel complete.

Susanne Wiggins Bunch

PERSPECTIVE

It's amazing the comfort I receive
lying on the floor back-to-back
with a big soft brown-haired
warm-bodied mutt named Sarge.

He never quite understands
why I enter his domain,
stoop to his level,
seek his companionship.

But I know he relishes it
as much as I do.
It's wonderful, feeling him relax
as I nuzzle closer.

This fierce protector of my safety
sleeps more soundly as years
rob him of his puppyhood. For these
few precious moments, we are young
and spring is in the air.

Mary Lenore Quigley

A DOG

'Tis pity not to have a dog,
    For at the long day's end
The man or boy will know the joy
    Of welcome from a friend.
And whether he be rich or poor
    Or much or little bring,
The dog will mark his step and bark
    As if he were a king.

Though gossips whisper now and then
    Of faults they plainly see,
And some may sneer, from year to year
    My dog stays true to me.
He's glad to follow where I go,
    And though I win or fail
His love for me he'll let me see
    By wagging of his tail.

Now if I were to list the friends
    Of mine in smiles and tears
Who through and through are staunch and true
    And constant down the years,

In spite of all my many faults
    Which critics catalog
Deserving blame, I'd have to name
    My ever-faithful dog.

'Tis pity not to have a dog,
    Whatever be his breed,
For dogs possess a faithfulness
    Which humans sadly need.
And whether skies be blue or gray,
    Good luck or ill attend
Man's toil by day, a dog will stay
    His ever-constant friend.

Edgar A. Guest

EVER FAITHFUL, EVER FRIENDS

Our canine friends remain.
They never waver from their chosen path.
In poverty and prosperity, in health and in sickness,
their loyalty stands firm and immovable.
They will fight all the elements to protect us from harm.
While we sleep soundly in the comfort of our homes
they guard us without question; providing a safe haven
within the circle of their devotion.
And when the fierce winds of the world
brush against our battered souls
they offer comfort to ease our fears.
They will follow us through all seasons.
They remain as strong and steady advocates.
Their simple thoughts are always turned
toward us, our happiness; our well-being.
They will never close the door to their hearts.
They remain always, without end.
Ever faithful. Ever friends.

Leslie A. Neilson

PLEASURE

The great pleasure of a dog is that you may make a fool of yourself with him and not only will he not scold you, but he will make a fool of himself too.

Samuel Butler

CHAPTER FOUR

Devotion

FURRY SHRINK

I'd double his life if I could —
we share a history.
When friends turn false, my dog stays true,
his head upon my knee.

He can erase my loneliness —
my pain melts in his eyes.
My dog lies close — he understands
what I cannot disguise.

Janet Lombard

DOG TRAINING

With arms wide open,
she received
her best gift ever
in her 12th year.
It was just in time.
The dark plain of
Teenage loomed before her.
The dog, her hero along a decade's pathless route,
would save her inside and out, over and over,
like a good trick.
Protection here
Devotion there.
Cavorting, adoring, rebounding, attending.
Teaching the basics she'd
miss everywhere else:
contentment,
exuberance,
reliability,
disdain for the disingenuous.
A cadre of skills

that would turn around twice
and curl up deep within her,
watchful, loyal,
serving for the duration.

Kate Dwyer

A NOTE FOR MY FIRST

Years ago, there was only you, itty, bitty you,
too small to climb the stairs or jump onto the sofa,
a bounding ball of fresh white fur, always at my heels as we
    explored the yard.

Times changed.
We banished you from upstairs and forbade you from the sofa.
You hit six months, and we installed a fence —
2 × 4s contain you, but not your high-pitched bark.

One baby came home, then another —
tough times for a terrier.
But babies become small people, which you seem to like,
especially when they bounce balls and hold running hoses.

Eight years old
and you still don't know when to yap, what to eat, where to pee.
No matter — you've mastered the big stuff,
like sniffing out evil and licking floors clean.
A child cries — you sprint to the scene.
An adult stews — you keep her company.
In your world, we all come first.

Yes, you deserve more walks, more rubs, more brushing, too.
I can't promise those, but I do promise this — we'll always
love you.

Kathleen Whitman Plucker

RESCUE

Dog,
you come to me
head held low,
tongue hanging out
the side of your mouth,
sad tales in your eyes.

Dog,
you come to me
from the highway,
frantic and pacing,
feet tough from walking,
ribs poking through rough fur.

Dog,
you come to me
a bundle of fear
barking at shadows,
growling at ghosts,
shrinking from monsters.

Dog,
you come to me
searching for something,
nudging my hand,
tentatively licking,
quiet and soft.

Dog,
you come to me
over and over.
I clean you up
then pass you on,
wait for the next one.

Karen R. Porter

HE KNEW

He knew
in those painful,
drawn-out minutes
before the ambulance's arrival
what you didn't know.

And what he knew
was exactly what you
needed,
all alone, except for him,
in the most excruciating
pain of your life,
fearing the worst.

He laid his head
on your arm and
gave you an unwavering
look that said,
"I'm here,
I'm not going anywhere."

Susan Koefod

A DOG'S LIFE

I wait and watch until
you come home from work
Most evenings worries
score your face like so many
over-gnawed dog bones

I jump and cavort around
while slowly that sad face
lowers down, lets me
lick all its trouble away

You laugh, I bark,
straight from my heart;
finally, a smile!
That's all it takes
to make my long, lonely
dog's day worthwhile

Arlene Gay Levine

THE GUARDIAN

He commands with gentleness that which he calls his own,

Ever vigilant, ever watchful, he reaches into the depths of his
soul and pours a thousand years of wisdom from his
knowing eyes.

In quiet repose he guards the darkness, his presence filling the
room, his bearing regal, his dignity unquestionable.

Powerful is the roar that fills the night if the peace and sanctity
of his beloved home is disturbed.

Yet, scratched on the belly he fills with delight, his sense of
humor tickled by the children he adores.

No more does he ask than to love and be loved in return. For
this alone will he lay down his life.

He teaches those things that can never be put into words, nor
understood by the faint of heart.

His lessons speak silently of unconditional love, fidelity, and
complete communion with nature, understood by so few
in this lifetime.

For those who love him, his dominion is complete, his heart
forever faithful.

Susan A. Krauser

GUIDE DOG

Each night, just before going to bed,
I enter the study and sit down
in the room's only straight-backed chair.
With my bare feet flat on the hardwood floor
and my palms resting lightly on my thighs,
I close my eyes and begin slowly to breathe:
pulling into my mind, my heart, my body,
as much of the world's abundance as I can:

May so-and-so be happy, may so-and-so be
healed, may so-and-so be . . .

My dog knows all of this, knows the routine.
And now she, too, enters the room.
Enters and lies down in the middle of the floor.
Even before I go in, she is there, settled and breathing.

Now, on those nights when I would prefer
to skip the routine altogether, from busyness or exhaustion,
I know that I cannot. Because there she is, waiting —

a reminder for me that there is work to do:
deep, prayerful work, there in the dark,
her breath and mine.

Lisa Dordal

MY COMFORTER

The world had all gone wrong that day
And tired and in despair,
Discouraged with the ways of life,
I sank into my chair.

A soft caress fell on my cheek,
My hands were thrust apart.
And two big sympathizing eyes
Gazed down into my heart.

I had a friend; what cared I now
For fifty worlds? I knew
One heart was anxious when I grieved —
My dog's heart, loyal, true.

"God bless him," breathed I soft and low,
And hugged him close and tight.
One lingering lick upon my ear
And we were happy — quite.

Author unknown

DEAR COMPANION

I've often walked you at dawn, when it was the darkest hour. We had crossed the fields, felt the breeze as a new day came shining through. The keenness of the wind so true brings back those memories when together, my wet-nosed friend, you and I had all the world to see. Up and up we went to tackle the hill, to soak our feet in the shimmering coldness of the morning dew. How can I thank you for what you meant to me? My thanks are but a drop in the ocean when they should be a million times larger than the sea. Thank you, my faithful pet, for the tireless loyalty you have given me through the years, and when I hold your collar and lead I cherish them, I can't help myself, with many a shake of the head and a quiet tear flowing from eyes too old to see. My dear companion so ill, but I'll remember you; I know I will.

Cleveland W. Gibson

CHAPTER FIVE

Aging Gracefully

OLD FRIENDS

Their youthful years have slipped away,
The old man and his dog.
They have a special bonding
That needs no dialogue.

The chase is just a memory,
But how they used to run
When hearts and legs were stronger
And games were such great fun.

Now the pace is slower
For the master and his mate.
If one lags too far behind
The other stops to wait.

Some things we cannot change
Like aging and the weather,
But true friends are quite content
Just growing old together.

C. David Hay

DOG WALK

The dog is old, muzzle frosted,
hips narrow and unruly.
Outings now are more meditation
than distance traveled,
more amble than cavort.

There was a time for bounding.
Leashes in impossible tangles.
He'd gallop past, ears laid back,
neck outstretched.
So much energy, we'd squander it
on capers measured in miles.

It is all about the stopping now.
He picks his way down the block,
back toes dragging just a little,
his nose reading every shrub,
each thicket of grass, leisurely,
like whole sections of the Sunday *Times*.
He sometimes pauses, mid-walk,
head lifted. Just stands there,
hips slightly swaying,

until I turn around to meet his gaze.
The very best part of him still working fine.

Kate Dwyer

MY ELDERLY DOG

"A brand new puppy? Oh, yes, sure!"
Not knowing what to think of,
We welcomed in that wiggly,
Boundless energy and love.

The years since then have melted,
With once-young child in college.
And dear dog, grown past vibrancy,
Is gentled now by age.

She's blind. She's deaf,
And for hours sleeps.
No longer licks our faces,
No more plays or leaps.

Yet her snore, her padding about,
And soft presence are balm, you see.
She simply "is," and reminds
Our souls to simply "be."

Gladly, we return to her what
All wish would never cease.

We give comfort, rest, security,
To crown her elder years with peace.

Donna J. Maebori

RESTRICTED TRAVEL

I descend the canyon just a little,
jumping boulders in the stream, but my dog,
my aging golden retriever, is none too good
at scrambling down. A drop of four, five feet
sets him barking fresh refusals. Now that he's almost

nine years old, he's given up alternate routes.
So he stands there, barking,
and I'm just a bit ahead, just getting to the better part,
where the channel steepens in pools and falls
and the canyon opens out of oaks and laurel

into sunshine. From here you can almost glimpse
the sea, the islands round the far horizon.
But I climb back into the shade and tell myself
that next time I will come alone, knowing I won't.
As I cradle him up by his quivering haunches,

or ease him out of a pool by his collar, I think
that this is why I came. And he stands on a tangle
of alder roots and shakes himself, and we

are very wet together, and this is how we share
the creek, this is how we bless the canyon.

Paul Willis

BESTY

He's an old dog now, with just three legs
and a coarse harsh wheeze
that rousts me out of sleep
the way a baby's crying stirs
uncertain rumors of another world.
He's near the edge of something that I think is death,
and as the world grows quiet all around him,
I'm troubled most by his tranquility.
Once anything that moved or smelled could make him burn,
but now he's even let go of desire,
like a kid who strings his name and address to a balloon,
and watches as it disappears above the trees and houses,
to wait for days for news from foreign towns that never
    comes;
now the morning sunlight in a warm red chair
and the leisurely savor of bitch on the wet guttered leaves
sustain him like prayer.

In his glory days he used to chase
airplanes across the yard, to race
in circles blind with joy around an apple tree

until his speed brought thinking to a standstill,
and his body blurred its outlines like the rising
sunlight buffeting a field of windy wheat,
or wind itself unthreading all the star-
entangled cirrus clouds that roam the moon like sheep
he must have known somehow to long for in a field
rock-ridged and sparse with heather, where the Hebrides
survey the ocean's tumult and the far gulls cry,
where he could circle, ride, and prod, and raucous until dark.

I want to shepherd him across the last dark frozen grasses
into the silence below zero
when the wind has been stunned by its own bitter summons
and stars stand fixed in their ice black arteries
and any breath at all might turn the world to smoke.
And in that instant's no-man's-land when time
rolls up its sleeves to show
that it has nothing left to hide, no sleights or tricks,
I can turn back
and let him take his way alone from there
by smell, and heart, and what remains of eye and ear.
I pack a final snowball full of stars
and toss it out to where the horizon flickers

and watch him go for it,
still game on three legs in the deep powder,
and call out after him
until the emptiness inside each syllable works free,
Great Besty! Go get it Boy! Great Besty! Good Boy! Goodby

William Shullenberger

HIKING OLD DOG TO THE ALPINE LAKE

She takes the lead with unaccustomed spryness,
remembering this route through sagebrush, bitterbrush,
mules-ears drying like so many summers
to a lake still blue, sky filtered through runoff snow.

Her lungs pump noisy on this once-a-year hike,
the only season this water gathers enough sun
for an old dog's joints. You'd never guess,
the way she chases sticks in the waves,
and we keep on throwing, remembering her a puppy.

Finally the old-dog sourness washes off
and her fetches turn to good-dog weariness.

And then we take it a slow walk back,
holding in so the old lady still can take the lead.
So slow, by the time we reach the car,
she smells of nothing but drying grasses,
lupine and sage.

Taylor Graham

OUR OLD DOG

On good days, he shows traces
of his younger self.
He's eager for a walk
and has a sprightly step.
He sniffs the air,
and cocks his head,
ready to explore our
neighborhood, his world.

On other days,
he's racked by a cough,
ballad of his failing heart.
Curled up in a slice of sunlight,
he seems smaller than
his thirteen pounds.
We huddle beside him,
stroke his white-flecked coat,
absorb his lessons on slipping away.

Ann Reisfeld Boutté

NEW TRICKS

The old dog's once-clear eyes,
now filled with his clouded destiny;
his aged body quickening towards
the familiar voice he cannot see,
rippling with quiet joy
that Love has called him,
once again;
his head nodding heavily
with reciprocated desire.

What joy should fill
God's waiting heart,
if from such trusting pets,
we humans could learn
not to ponder our worthiness
to be loved,
but chose instead the uninhibited,
slobbering joy of a lesser creature
anticipating the affection
of his Master.

Sally Clark

TO LET YOU GO GENTLY

To all things come an end, it's said
But I am not yet ready to surrender
Your soul to that cold night.
Part of me prays
That you won't want to leave us, too soon,
But I know it's a kind of selfishness
As I watch your painful step
And see you labor to move stiff joints in the morning.
So I give thanks for every day
That you show the joy of life still —
Rolling and scrubbing in the grass in the back yard,
Barking at your dog-buddies,
Brandishing one of your well-worn chew-toys
With that old-time glint in your eyes.
And I pray to the higher power
To grant me, when That Time arrives,
The courage to look in your eyes
And read truly what is written there
And let you go gently
When it's time.

Lisa Timpf

HIS FINAL SEASON

After the thunder has stopped, Bentley still trembles. I coax him outside because it smells like spring and he will not live to see another. As thick blankets of clouds smother the sun, we roam the sodden yard, searching for a stick. When I find one that isn't too heavy, I watch him amble after it, then settle down to chew it to shreds. He has never been much of a retriever.

Then the clouds blow apart and I see the sun so bright it makes my eyes wet, knowing I'll have to face the next thunderstorm alone.

Arlene L. Mandell

OLD DOG

When her rabies tag arrived in the mail
I tossed it on the kitchen counter.
She won't jump the wall
Or jerk the leash from my hand and bolt.

Years ago she disappeared on our morning walk
An elegant black streak on the first white-hot day of summer
Lured up a hill from the arroyo
By a deer, a rabbit, the irresistible, dizzying scent of freedom.
That night, certain the desert had claimed her
I struggled to let go
But at dawn, her coat matted, trailing cactus,
She rolled into the kitchen when I opened the door.
Grinning, she drained her water dish and collapsed on the tile
To sleep off her foolishness.

This morning she staggers to her feet, rear end listing oddly,
And hangs back, though we walk only to the end of the street.
She cannot see the rabbit dart directly in front of her
From its cover of rock and desert broom,
Does not respond to the repeated yelp
Of the alarm on the neighbor's car.

At home again, I pick up her tag and work the stiff metal ring
    apart
Forcing it onto her collar
As if a simple act of will, a talisman
Can hold back time.

Nancy B. Wall

CHAPTER SIX

Partings

A GOODBYE PRAYER

Bless my friend who's gone away
I honor him this lonely day.

Lift my friend on wings of love
To Heaven lit with cheerful sun.

Dry my tears and soothe this pain
Let my world be whole again.

Kate Robinson

IF IT SHOULD BE

If it should be that I grow weak
And pain should keep me from my sleep,
Then you must do what must be done,
For this last battle cannot be won.

You will be sad, I understand.
Don't let your grief then stay your hand.
For this day, more than all the rest,
Your love for me must stand the test.

We've had so many happy years.
What is to come can hold no fears.
You'd not want me to suffer so;
The time has come — please let me go.

Take me where my need they'll tend,
And please stay with me till the end.
Hold me firm and speak to me,
Until my eyes no longer see.

I know in time that you will see
The kindness that you did for me.

Although my tail its last has waved,
From pain and suffering I've been saved.

Please do not grieve — it must be you
Who had this painful thing to do.
We've been so close, we two, these years;
Don't let your heart hold back its tears.

Author unknown

RAINBOW BRIDGE

Just this side of heaven is a place called Rainbow Bridge. When animals die that have been especially close to someone here, they go to Rainbow Bridge. There are meadows and hills for all our special friends so they can run and play together. There is plenty of food, water, and sunshine, and our friends are warm and comfortable.

All the animals who have been ill and old are restored to health and vigor; those who were hurt or maimed are made whole and strong again, just as we remember them in our dreams of days and times gone by. The animals are happy and content, except for one small thing: they each miss someone very special to them, who had to be left behind.

They all run and play together, but the day comes when one suddenly stops and looks into the distance. His bright eyes are intent; his eager body begins to quiver. Suddenly he begins to run from the group, flying over the green grass, his legs carrying him faster and faster. You have been spotted, and when you and your special friend finally meet, you cling together in joyous reunion, never to be parted again. The happy kisses rain upon your face; your hands again caress the beloved head, and you look once more into the trusting eyes of your pet, so long gone from your life but never absent from your heart.

Then you cross Rainbow Bridge together.

Author unknown

SUMMERHILL, AUGUST 1, 2003

For Niki

Fourteen and a half years
this hillside
sweet greens of spring
sleeping in the shade
path walks in autumn's tang
the snows you loved —
one hundred and one in dog years,
they say.

We ponder your simplicity —
one suit of clothing
for all seasons
no pockets
no purse
no stash under the mattress.
You owned one bowl
one toothbrush
one collar and leash —
and us.

Judy Kolosso

CEREMONY AT DAWN

We are bundled to each other
under the plate of a frosty moon
hung against the flush of first light.
Elegizing, we remember days
our beloved dog ran circles
with the children who first chose her
as a fluffy puff of tongue and fur,
the children she met each day
with raised nose and whopping tail.
The air so brittle words break
into the tears of friendship's end,
grateful for the honor of the task,
we dig, heaving with the sacred work
of letting go. As we bend to lift the old dog
cold from death's grip, we release her
and our years of gratitude
like a prayer under the shared gaze
of a dawning sun and a silent holy moon.

Anne McCrady

BEST FRIENDS

I had a dog and he had me,
We were the best of company.
He was my shadow, loyal and true,
Where I went he followed too.

I was the master — always there
Who gave him kind and loving care.
He was the friend I treasured so —
When I was down he seemed to know.

But he grew old before my time,
Lagging now in step and climb.
I slowed my pace to match his gait
But often had to stop and wait.

If he could, he'd follow still.
He broke my heart — as old dogs will.
I miss the eyes that shone to say
He'd love me till his dying day.

I oft forget and reach to touch
The old gray head I miss so much;

Wishing for the time again —
When he had me and I had him.

C. David Hay

ELLIOTT AND AMELIA

When my parents' beloved German shorthaired pointer, Elliott, died last year, all of us mourned. He had been my father's best friend.

Amelia, my two-year-old, does not move through the stages of grief like the rest of us, so for her, Elliott is still alive. She looks for him when we visit. Last time, when she sat down to color in my parents' den, she took a framed picture of Elliott they keep beside the new fish tank and stood it up next to the crayons. "Sit together," she told me, pointing to the picture.

The attachment surprises me because we did not see Elliott very often (my parents live several states away), and Amelia's young attention span is capricious. But she remembers everything about Elliott. She laughs about his kisses, and points to her hand where he liked to lick. She says "Elliott" every time she sees a squirrel, because he liked to chase them, and she always asks about him when she gets on the phone with my parents.

Instead of saying he's "night-night" or in Heaven, like we once did, we allow his memory to live, and we laugh along with my little girl when we talk about the pooch. My favorite picture is one of them together — black-and-white-patched Elliott and my bald little baby who had just learned to walk, sitting on the floor with their heads together.

"Friends," she says, pointing to that photo.
Friends.

Cari Oleskewicz

IF THIS WERE EGYPT

Below a wet April sky John dug your grave,
the lilac blossoms above it
just small thoughts kept to themselves.

We carried your body and laid you down
in that bowl of brown earth where you curled
clean and white, a wolf, sleeping.

To take on your journey we put biscuits and cheese
and slim crocus petals which the boy
who knew you his whole life
dropped in with shaking hands.

If this were Egypt, best good dog,
we wouldn't stop there —
adding one pizza delivery guy in a red cap;
a UPS driver, the one with blond hair
springing from his head like corn straw;
the whistling meter reader you couldn't quite reach
through the wooded teeth of fence; two smart-assed
kids on mountain bikes; one young plumber
with a tool belt; the doorbell with wiring attached;

three squirrels, one grackle, a raccoon,
and, if possible, the neighbor's slinking cat.

Lisa Zimmerman

THE LAST TIME

I hold her across my lap
my face buried
in her curled black fur
breathing in
her familiar dog scent.
I finger her green woven collar
still warm with her.
I stroke her arthritic little body
stiffening in my arms.
The oil in my fingers
the oily residue of my tears
anoint her for the last time.

Donna Wahlert

RETRIEVER

"Imagination is the great retriever."
— Charles Wright

If "Heaven is a lovely lake of beer," as St. Bridget wrote,
then dog heaven must be this tub of kibble, where you can push
your muzzle all day long without getting bloat or bellyache.
Where every toilet seat is raised, at the right level
for slurping, and fire hydrants and saplings tell you, "Here.
Relieve yourself on us." And the sun and moon
fall at your feet, celestial Frisbees flinging themselves
in shining arcs for your soft mouth to retrieve. Rumi says,
"Personality is a small dog trying to get the soul to play,"
but you are a big dog, with an even larger heart, and you
have redeemed our better selves. Forgive us for the times
we walked away, wanted to do taxes or wash dishes
instead of playing fetch or tugger. In the green field
of heaven, there are no collars, no leashes, no delivery trucks
with bad brakes, and all the dogs run free. Barking is allowed,
and every pocket holds a treat. Sit. Stay. Good dog.

Barbara Crooker

THE POWER OF THE DOG

There is sorrow enough in the natural way
From men and women to fill our day;
And when we are certain of sorrow in store,
Why do we always arrange for more?
Brothers and Sisters, I bid you beware
Of giving your heart to a dog to tear.

Buy a pup and your money will buy
Love unflinching that cannot lie —
Perfect passion and worship fed
By a kick in the ribs or a pat on the head.
Nevertheless it is hardly fair
To risk your heart for a dog to tear.

When the fourteen years which Nature permits
Are closing in asthma, or tumour, or fits,
And the vet's unspoken prescription runs
To lethal chambers or loaded guns,
Then you will find — it's your own affair —
But . . . you've given your heart to a dog to tear.
When the body that lived at your single will,
With its whimper of welcome, is stilled (how still!)

When the spirit that answered your every mood
Is gone — wherever it goes — for good,
You will discover how much you care,
And will give your heart to a dog to tear.

We've sorrow enough in the natural way,
When it comes to burying Christian clay.
Our loves are not given, but only lent,
At compound interest of cent per cent.
Though it is not always the case, I believe,
That the longer we've kept 'em, the more do we grieve:
For, when debts are payable, right or wrong,
A short-time loan is as bad as a long —
So why in — Heaven (before we are there)
Should we give our hearts to a dog to tear?

Rudyard Kipling

DOG MEMORIAL

We have come here today to honor and give thanks for a very special dog, [*dog's name*]. This creature of God holds a very special place in the hearts of the people gathered together here today. [*Dog's name*] made her* transition on [*date*], and we come here to mark her passing with a remembering of the gift she was and the gifts she brought into the lives she touched. You who have come here today to remember [*dog's name*] are here because your life was no doubt made richer and fuller by having known this special furry loved one. Anyone who has had the honor of having a dog knows what it feels like to be trusted completely, forgiven immediately, and loved unconditionally.

I would like to invite any of you who would feel comfortable doing so to share with us for a few moments whatever memories you would like to share.

[*Allow time for sharing.*]

Thank you each for sharing your memories with us. God is love and God is life. We gathered here know that certainly [*dog's name*] is an expression of God's love and life. Though she is not here physically any longer, her essence, which is love, will always be with you.

Let us pray.

Blessed Mother/Father Creator of all,

We give grateful thanks for [*dog's name*].

---

* For a male dog, substitute the appropriate masculine pronouns throughout.

We give thanks that she came wagging her tail
  into the lives of her friends and family
  and by so doing made their lives richer and fuller.
We hold her memory lovingly in our hearts
  as we have released her physical form.
We give thanks for the lessons she taught so
  patiently and lovingly.
We are grateful for the time we were together in this life
  and know that the essence of [*dog's name*] lives on,
  for her essence is love.
As we grieve her passing we celebrate her life.
We give thanks that she chose [*owner's name*]
  to be her people and in choosing them
  became an important member of their family.
Being the people chosen by [*dog's name*] is a blessing
  that even now calls us to come up higher, to forgive more
  quickly, trust more easily, and love unconditionally.
Thank you, God, for your love so wonderfully
  expressed in the being of [*dog's name*].
We release our loved one into the care of a loving God. Amen.

Rev. Gloria S. Moncrief

CHAPTER SEVEN

Reflections

DOGS ARE OUR LINK TO PARADISE

Dogs are our link to paradise. They don't know evil or jealousy or discontent. To sit with a dog on a hillside on a glorious afternoon is to be back in Eden, where doing nothing was not boring — it was peace.

Milan Kundera

POEM FOR A LOST DOG

I see your face every day
Watching hopefully from your place on the telephone pole
Seeking, searching for a savior
To bring you back where you belong

You prance through my thoughts
On well-worn paws
White tail wagging, waving its surrender, its SOS
Calling "Come find me, O Good Samaritan"

Months march on
Autumn's gentle leaves turn to winter's floating flakes
Your flier, your face, ever-fading, growing fainter
Until the wayward wanderer becomes a whisper

At night you still dance through my dreams
I wonder, where have you gone?
Did your redeemer rescue you?
Then I bow my head, and fervently pray

That somehow, some day you found your way

Home

Teri Wilson

IF YOU DON'T OWN A DOG

If you don't own a dog, at least one, there is not necessarily anything wrong with you, but there may be something wrong with your life.

Roger Caras

HIGHER POWER

You let the transformative power
of unconditional love enter
your life: you bought a Dog.

So thou shalt not ignore
the one who adores you!
Pet, pamper, play

and laugh with your loyal fan, grateful
for the comfort and companionship
only they can provide.

After all, everyone knows
Dog is just another way
to spell God.

Arlene Gay Levine

THE MEANING OF LOVE

Nobody can fully understand the meaning of love unless he's owned a dog. A dog can show you more honest affection with a flick of his tail than a man can gather through a lifetime of handshakes.

Gene Hill

THE NATURE OF HIS KNOWING

He knows somehow
The exact moment I am coming to bed.
There is never a false alarm on his part.
Before I rise from the chair.
He leaves my side of the bed
And moves to the floor to round himself in place.

Some nights I call him back to bed
To lie beside me,
To touch fur,
To hear his soft animal breathing.

This night I enter in darkness
And make my way to his bed.
I kneel and give thanks to this body of motion,
This creature of hair and bone.
I stroke his ears and whisper a blessing
For the nature of his knowing,
For the gifts he freely gives.

Dan Vera

MY DAUGHTER'S FIRST WORD

Dog.

Everything
was Dog.

The crib,
the cat,
the wall.

Even the dog
was Dog.

Dog this.
Dog that.

Dog!
Dog!
Dog!

Stuck out my tongue
just so I'd be called

Dog.

To be counted
as just one of the many

dogs

in my daughter's
doggy-dog world.

Peter Markus

BLIZZARD

Summer mornings the Spitz
would appear on the front porch —
me settled in with coffee, books,

notebook — and like a familiar prayer
both ask and receive: blessing
me, wanting petting, and then

lie — stunning white, against red
porch floor — quiet as a still life
but breathing steady, rhythmic.

God pouring from his heart and
lungs. "Good dog."

Barbara Schmitz

LESSONS FROM DOGS

Dogs have become a part of our family and a part of our personal history. They live in the house with us; they sit and sleep together with us. They have brought something unique and satisfying to our lives. They have loved us unconditionally and have taught us important lessons for better living — how to embrace life, how to enjoy the moment, how to let go when it's time to let go, even when it seems way too soon. They have taught us that the only thing of permanence in life is love and that to spend life rejoicing in its opportunities and its mystery is better than to spend life adding to its misery and sorrow.

Bernard S. Siegel, MD

CARING FOR A SICK DOG

Wrapped in my sleeping bag
by the side of your wicker basket,
I listen for your slightest whimper.
When you stir in your sleep,
I reach out to soothe you —
fingers through shaggy fur
touching your ribs
feeling your heartbeat.

Donna Wahlert

SHORT LIVES

I have sometimes thought of the final cause of dogs having such short lives and I am quite satisfied it is in compassion to the human race; for if we suffer so much in losing a dog after an acquaintance of ten or twelve years, what would it be if they were to live double that time?

Sir Walter Scott

LESSONS LEARNED POST-9/11

Rev. Roberta Finkelstein reflects on lessons learned
from her dog in the wake of the 9/11 terrorist attacks.

Enthusiasm and engagement. That is the spirituality of the dog. . . . My dog Pepper loves me absolutely, he thinks I'm wonderful all the time, and he is absolutely enthusiastic about the world.

The word *enthusiasm* has an interesting root. It goes back to the Greek *en theos* — the indwelling of God. Enthusiasm is not mindless; it is a deep and abiding belief in the goodness of life. That's the spirituality of the dog — engaged with the world, out there seeing and smelling and interacting. And constantly affirming its basic goodness. . . .

On September 12th, when I woke up the day after, exhausted from a mostly sleepless night and wondering how I could possibly prepare for the services I had promised that evening, it was Pepper who helped me get back my perspective.

For Pepper, the morning after September 11 was a morning like any other. He charged up from his bed, headed straight for the door, wriggled in anticipation while I hooked on his leash, then charged out the door and down the porch steps. Oh, those first sniffs at the bushes! Ah, that first whiff of green grass. Always we go past the first couple of houses with his nose buried in the delicious smells of the neighborhood. Then, as we approach the mini-park, he stops and looks back at me. "Isn't this great?" he asks, tail wagging. "Can you believe it's all still here?"

I don't know which was harder to believe that morning. That the Twin Towers were gone, that the seemingly impregnable Pentagon walls had been breached. Unbelievable! Or was it even more unbelievable what Pepper told me that morning? That it — the grass, the bushes, the familiar smells and stops along our regular morning route — it was all still there in all its glory.

Pepper doesn't know much about terrorism or foreign policy. But what he does know is that all that was right and wonderful and dependable about our life on September 10th is still here. He knows it because of his enthusiasm for life — his ability to embody the indwelling of goodness and rightness. He teaches me, every morning, a most important lesson: be uncomplicated, be genuine, be glad to be alive. Because (sniff) it's all still here!

Rev. Roberta Finkelstein

CHAPTER EIGHT

Prayers, Blessings, and Inspiration

DOGGY PRAYER

I am grateful, my four-legged friend,
for shared treasures — earth, sky, and sea,
for shared pleasure — a winter's nap, a frolic,
a drink from a mountain spring.

While you do not speak my language,
nor I your guttural tongue,
I know that you, too, feel our spirits
merging into One.

I offer you this blessing
as you face the setting sun:
May you always know adventure
and the peace of going home.

Kate Robinson

She was taken from a wild pack in Queens. Something indefinable about her kept the ASPCA officers from euthanizing her right away.* And then, realizing she was not vicious and that she was pregnant, they asked my friend Erika (who used to work at the ASPCA) if she would foster this shepherd-chow mix until the pups were born and weaned, warning her not to get attached; a dog with her history almost always has to be put down.

Erika named her Zoë, found homes for all her puppies, and together, they went to class: obedience, advanced obedience, agility, and all the courses required for Zoë to be certified as a therapy dog.

They could now make regular visits to a retirement home for priests. The priests and the nurses were all happy to see this beautiful dog. Even the old fellow who, when she first started visiting, would dash into his room and slam the door, yelling, "I like cats!" was won over when Erika told him that Zoë liked cats, too — she lived with four of them.

One of the residents was confined to a wheelchair and, because of Alzheimer's, lost to the world around him. The nurses told Erika that he spent most days screaming. No one could reach him anymore — except Zoë.

---

* The packs must be culled periodically; if they get too large they become dangerous. Most of the dogs captured must be euthanized because they are diseased or too wild to be adopted (no facilities to care for feral dogs exist in New York).

When he saw her coming toward him down the corridor, he became quiet and recognition would light his eyes. When she rested her muzzle on his knee, he stroked her head and spoke her name. In her presence, he experienced a glimmer of lucidity, a moment of connection and peace.

This is a dog blessing a priest.

Paulette Callen

DOG OWNER'S PRAYER

Lord, thank you for this ornery mutt
who thinks I'm royalty and more.
Bless wag of tail, each woof and bark,
each mark of slobber on the door.

Once house and rugs were fragrance free.
Keep me mindful of those days:
No welcome whiff of doggy breath,
no Eau du After Rain to praise.

Restore my grateful, patient heart
for this, the dearest of ankle-nippers,
and keep me ever watchful, Lord —
at least until I find my slippers.

Sandra Soli

PRAYER FOR MY BEST FRIEND

Bless his nose, so wet and cold
Bless his fur, so soft to hold.
Bless his tail, it wags so strong
When I tell him he may come along.
Bless those ears that stand so stout
Except when one's turned inside out.
Bless those eyes so filled with love
That surely comes from God above.
For up in Heaven the Angels sing,
They fly with harps on silver wings.
But here on Earth there can be no doubt,
The Angels bark as they run about.

Brennan Boyle,
age 12

A BLESSING

Though it was a quiet Sunday afternoon the park was spilling over with people and dogs. Dewey, still a pup, put his paws up on the dashboard to see what was going on, just as I spotted a sign that read *Blessing of the Animals*.

The park was embellished with newly fallen leaves that glowed like the amber-colored stained glass in the church's high windows. As I stepped onto the lawn and saw two-leggeds and four-leggeds moving in tandem over the rounded hills, I felt like we'd wandered into the Garden of Eden.

In that moment, which felt like a long-forgotten memory, I could see how animals embody love. They snuggle up against us at night, or bump us with a wet nose for a pat. The dogs we care for remind us of our connection with the Earth — the here and now. They pull ahead, snout pressed to the turf, as we dangle from the other end of a leash. And we are stopped temporarily in our busy tracks as they sniff the grass around a street sign. They get us down on the floor to romp with a tug toy, and whether it's in a twentieth-floor condominium or a one-story rambler we're closer to the Earth beneath us.

The celebration of life that they model every day helps us remember that we too can live in the present moment. Like St. Francis, with birds perched on his hands and foxes at his feet, we have the potential to become one with all creation.

Milissa Link

DOG BLESSING

We pray to you, God, our Creator, to bless our dogs with Your radiant light and love. May our animal friends have good health and happy lives and always be protected and safe.

We ask for better understanding as we learn from our dogs' wisdom, their innocence, their loyalty and particularly their seeming ability to not judge human beings unkindly.

Thank you for the pleasures, playfulness, and sometimes the surprising humor our pets display.

Thank you for their companionship and friendship, especially for those lonely hours we may have experienced.

Thank you for our companions' natural ability to teach us to be aware of the present moment.

Thank you for the pure beauty of every dog — their form, color, texture, motion is all a work of art, and may we appreciate Your creation of this masterpiece.

Bless all dogs in harm's way, heal the sick, protect those who are lost, and guide them to safety.

Thank you for the gift of love. Amen

Rev. Phyllis Ann Min

VOICES FROM THE SHELTER

(These are impressions of dogs I met
while volunteering at an animal shelter.)

I'm young and handsome and full of life,
Jumping and barking. I have so much to say!
A wire cage is no place for me! Can't you see that?
I would add so much to your life.
Give me a chance! Take me! Take me!

I'm not so handsome as the others, I'm far from perfect,
But they tell me that's just because I wasn't fed right.
I'm better now. Look, I can almost stand upright.
See how hard I try? I'll be the best dog once I'm well.
I'll soon be able to walk beside you, perhaps even run in front
     of you.
Inside, I'm the same kind of dog as all the others. I want what
     they want.
Do you want me? Take me!

I've been around the block a time or two,
Perhaps even three or four.
I may not have that many more spins in me, but I'm still here.
I'll wait for my drink, thankful that someone remembered

To put a rug in the bottom of my cage.
That's a comfort to old bones.
I can't see as well as I once did, but I can see a kind face
And sense at least a passing interest in me.
I won't rattle the bars, takes too much energy.
But I'll wag my tail for you to remind you
That someone once loved me very much, and I him,
And I still have love to give. Do you need some? Take me.

Rusty Hancock

I DEPEND ON YOU

I depend on you to feed me
substantially each day.
And when I am not sleeping
to know it's time to play.

I depend on you to pet me
when I nuzzle up your hand.
And accept my sloppy kisses
for the back rubs I demand.

I depend on you to walk with me
several times each day
to limber up our aging bones
that splinter and decay.

I depend on you to squeeze me
quite often 'round my neck
and roughly scratch behind my ears
and give my nose a peck.

But when my happy time is gone
or should you hear me cry...

I depend on you to love me most
when it's time to say goodbye.

Mary Lenore Quigley

3 A.M. FEEDING

Zeke grumbles and nudges
my door. Then I hear his claws
tapping toward my bed.
In the wash of moonlight
his black face gleams level with mine,
the large jaw politely closed, the eyes wide open.
I know what he wants. Yesterday

he found a nest of kittens on the side of the road
and though I can't hear them mewing, he can.
I'm too old for this, I think
as I throw on a robe and heat a cup of milk.
What am I doing saving cats
the world has too many of anyway?

The scraps of fur are trembling
on their skinny legs. It's all they can do
to hold up the globe of their heads.
Their eyes are oozing, swollen shut.
Two take the dropper, but the smallest
doesn't want to eat at all, opens
her mouth only to cry. Her tongue

is the size of a baby's thumbnail,
and petal thin. I pry apart
the tiny splinter teeth and squirt a little milk,
most of which leaks back out. Meanwhile

Zeke is in the zone, nabbing
each one as it wobbles, blindly
into his sphere. He's serene
as a massive star, culling stray bits of matter
that wander into his gravitational field.
One at a time, he pins them with a leaden
paw and sets about their baths
with his dry, relentless tongue.
He's been at it all day, trotting
back and forth, a zealous waiter,
anxious to bring whatever's required.

As I top off the last kitten, Zeke
goes at the bottoms of the others, as their mother
would do, urging them to deliver,
licking up the miniature excretions.
And when they're all finally settled
in the great warm arc of his body, he sighs
and lets his eyelids drift down with satisfaction.

I shuffle back to bed with a prayer:
Let me be like Zeke. Let me rush
to each moment with his devotion,
eager to lick even the underside of life.

Ellen Bass

I HAVE BROUGHT MY DOGS TO THE WOODS

It is autumn, and one of them, the big red male,
runs on ahead, rushing and leaping
up and down the decorated hills,
black tongue trembling, eyes rolling in his head.
But the other, the little one, the half-blind female,
sticks close to my heels, so that when I slow,
even a little, she stumbles into me,
and when I stop, she looks up at me
with her one good eye, and smiles.
Above my head I hear the sound of going,
and looking up, I see the high tops of the white oaks
bow, as though a presence travels by.
A shard splits off the sun, drops through the trees,
and sets the fallen leaves ablaze with shattered light.
Then I lift up my voice and say,
It is good to be here, to be rushing, wild, exultant,
or to be stumbling, smiling, only half blind.

Joanna Catherine Scott

LESSONS

If I greeted everyone happily
    Instead of eyeing with distrust
If I didn't pass judgment
    But accepted all
If I listened intently
    With understanding in my eyes
If I brought comfort
    All the time, no matter what
If I loved unconditionally
    Without reservation
If I lived life more simply
    Instead of worrying so much
If I played tirelessly
    And didn't work so hard
If I made people smile
    Just by my presence in the room
If I experienced true joy
    At the little things in life
Then I'd be the perfect friend
    Just like my dog.

Joanne Hirase-Stacey

DOGS AS SPIRITUAL MESSENGERS

I believe all creatures are God's masterpieces, but I also think most members of the human race could use some spiritual touching up by the artist. Dogs definitely play a part as spiritual messengers to help with that touch-up. Dogs are healers. They are enlightened. They seem to have figured out how to live beautifully so much better than we humans have. While we struggle to figure out why we were put here on Earth, all a dog wants is to love and be loved — a powerful lesson for us all.

Bernard S. Siegel, MD

Sources and Permission Acknowledgments

Grateful acknowledgment is made to the authors and publishers for the use of the following material. Every effort has been made to contact original sources. If notified, the publishers of this book will be pleased to rectify an omission in future editions.

Joan Marie Arbogast for "Puppy Dog Welcome."
Ellen Bass for "3 A.M. Feeding" and "Lost Dog." "Lost Dog" was previously published in *The Human Line* (Port Townsend, WA: Copper Canyon, 2007). Copyright © 2007 by Ellen Bass. Used with the permission of Copper Canyon Press, www.copper canyonpress.org. Ellen Bass's website is www.EllenBass.com.
John Bennett for "Walkies." Previously published in *Poems for Dog Lovers* (Nashville: Ideals Books, 2003).

Ann Reisfeld Boutté for "Our Old Dog."

Brennan Boyle for "Prayer for My Best Friend."

Susanne Wiggins Bunch for "Our Dog" and "Queen of Canine Capers."

Samuel Butler for "Pleasure," from *The Note-Books of Samuel Butler*, edited by Henry Festing Jones (London: A. C. Fifield, 1912; reprint, Charleston, SC: BiblioBazaar, 2006), 227.

Paulette Callen for "The Blessing."

Roger Caras for "If You Don't Own a Dog."

Kelly Cherry for "Mother of Dog."

Sally Clark for "New Tricks."

SuzAnne C. Cole for "Outside, Wanting In."

Ginny Lowe Connors for "Unleashed."

Barbara Crooker for "Retriever." Previously published in *Rock & Sling* (Fall/Winter 2006). www.BarbaraCrooker.com

Lisa Dordal for "Guide Dog" and "Sweeter Than Honey."

Fran Dorf for "What? Your Dog Doesn't Talk?" www.FranDorf.com

Kate Dwyer for "Dog Training" and "Dog Walk." www.BellaToccaTags.com

Joanne Esser for "Dog Running with His Man."

Janice A. Farringer for "Comfort Zone."

Rev. Roberta Finkelstein for "Lessons Learned Post-9/11," from *Blessing the Animals*, edited by Lynn L. Caruso (Woodstock,

VT: SkyLight Paths, 2006), 146–47. Reprinted by permission of Rev. Roberta Finkelstein. www.southchurch-uu.org

CB Follett for "At Limantour Beach" and "Off the Trail." "At Limantour Beach" was previously published in *Estero: A West Marin Quarterly*. "Off the Trail" was previously published as "Fresh Air After Rain" in *Sirius Verse*, edited by Bradley R. Strahan and Shirley Sullivan (Arlington, VA: Black Dog Press, 1998).

Cleveland W. Gibson for "Dear Companion."

Taylor Graham for "Hiking Old Dog to the Alpine Lake." Previously published in *Embers* (1991).

Edgar A. Guest for "A Dog," from *Collected Verse of Edgar A. Guest* (Chicago: Reilly & Lee, 1934), 715–16.

Rusty Hancock for "Voices from the Shelter."

C. David Hay for "Best Friends" and "Old Friends."

Gene Hill for "The Meaning of Love."

Joanne Hirase-Stacey for "Lessons."

Christine Otto Hirshland for "Homecoming."

Stephanie N. Johnson for "Skijoring with Kane."

Rudyard Kipling for "The Power of the Dog," from *Rudyard Kipling: Complete Verse, Definitive Edition* (New York: Anchor/Doubleday, 1989), 594–95. Copyright © 1940 by Elsie Kipling Bambridge.

Susan Koefod for "He Knew."

Judy Kolosso for "Summerhill, August 1, 2003." Previously published in *Stone Kettle Poets*.

Susan A. Krauser for "The Guardian."

Milan Kundera for "Dogs Are Our Link to Paradise," quoted in *Planet Dog*, edited by Sandra and Harry Choron (New York: Houghton Mifflin, 2005), 15.

Arlene Gay Levine for "A Dog's Life" and "Higher Power."

Sonya R. Liehr for "Rescue Dog."

Milissa Link for "A Blessing," an excerpt from her forthcoming memoir, *Dog Ma*.

Janet Lombard for "Furry Shrink."

Donna J. Maebori for "My Elderly Dog."

Arlene L. Mandell for "His Final Season."

Peter Markus for "My Daughter's First Word."

Lynn Martin for "Companions."

Anne McCrady for "Ceremony at Dawn." Previously published in *Encore*, the annual collection of prizewinners of the National Federation of State Poetry Societies (NFSPS), Inc. (2004). Anne McCrady's website is www.InSpiritry.com.

Nancy A. Messinger for "Dog Days."

Rev. Phyllis Ann Min for "Dog Blessing." www.phylliswithjoy.com

Rev. Gloria S. Moncrief for "Dog Memorial," from *Blessing the Animals*, edited by Lynn L. Caruso (Woodstock, VT: SkyLight

Paths, 2006), 208–10. Reprinted by permission of Rev. Gloria
S. Moncrief.

Leslie A. Neilson for "Ever Faithful, Ever Friends."
www.IlluminatedQuill.com

Eric Nelson for "Good Dog."

Joan Noëldechen for "The Greeting."

Cari Oleskewicz for "Elliott and Amelia."

Linda Opyr for "His."

Rosanne Osborne for "When Dogs Go Astray."

Kathleen Whitman Plucker for "A Note for My First."

Karen R. Porter for "Daisy" and "Rescue."

Mary Lenore Quigley for "I Depend on You" and "Perspective."

Kate Robinson for "A Goodbye Prayer" and "Doggy Prayer." "A
Goodbye Prayer" was previously published in *Bless the Beasts*,
edited by June Cotner (New York: SeaStar, 2002).

Millie Ruesch for "Love at First Sight."

Barbara Schmitz for "Blizzard."

Joanna Catherine Scott for "I Have Brought My Dogs to the
Woods." www.JoannaCatherineScott.com

Sir Walter Scott for "Short Lives," from *Blessing the Animals*, edited by Lynn L. Caruso (Woodstock, VT: SkyLight Paths,
2006), 15.

William Shullenberger for "Besty."

Bernard S. Siegel, MD, for "Dogs as Spiritual Messengers" and

"Lessons from Dogs," from *The Lazy Dog's Guide to Enlightenment*, edited by Andrea Hurst and Beth Wilson (Novato, CA: New World Library, 2007), 7–9. Reprinted by permission of Bernard S. Siegel, MD. www.BernieSiegelMD.com

Joan I. Siegel for "Dog Outside a Grocery on Broadway."

Sandra Soli for "Dog Owner's Prayer."

Patti Tana for "The Science of Faith." www.PattiTana.com

Lisa Timpf for "To Let You Go Gently."

Dan Vera for "The Nature of His Knowing." www.DanVera.com

Donna Wahlert for "Caring for a Sick Dog" and "The Last Time."

Nancy B. Wall for "Old Dog." Previously published in *Dog Music: Poetry about Dogs*, edited by Joseph Duemer and Jim Simmerman (New York: St. Martin's, 1997). "Old Dog" copyright © 1994 by Nancy B. Wall. Used by permission.

Louise Webster for "Puppy Days."

Paul Willis for "Higher Learning" and "Restricted Travel."

Teri Wilson for "Poem for a Lost Dog." www.TeriWilson.net

Lisa Zimmerman for "If This Were Egypt."

Author Index

About June Cotner

June Cotner is the author or editor of twenty-five books, including the bestselling *Graces*, *Bedside Prayers*, and *House Blessings*. June has appeared on the television programs *Northwest Afternoon* and *AM Northwest*. A graduate of the University of California at Berkeley, June teaches workshops throughout the country on a variety of subjects. She is the mother of two grown children and lives in Poulsbo, Washington, with her husband and two senior dogs (a golden oldie and a mischievous black Lab mix). Her hobbies include hiking, clogging, and playing with her two grandchildren. For more information, please visit www.JuneCotner.com.